ESSAYS ON
Everything

From the Sublime to the Ridiculous
With a Little in Between

MARGARET STORTZ

Table of Contents

On Chocolate

My love for chocolate is shameless...shameless, and I don't even care who knows it anymore. If I am addicted to the luscious brown stuff, what is the big deal? Believe me, there are worse dependencies in life than having to monitor one's daily chocolate intake! I think that there is actually something deeply spiritual about it. Whenever I take a bite of a bit of cacao, it wraps itself around the inside of my mouth, filling me with guilty pleasure, and causing the brain to think, "more, more!" Whenever I pass an upscale confectioner's shop with the windows lined with chocolate wrapped in gilt paper, I have to resist the temptation to genuflect. In fact the Rocky Mountain Chocolate Factory has used the motto: Never too rich, never too thin, never too much chocolate. I heartily concur. One out of three isn't bad, I guess.

When did this great love for chocolate begin, I can't even remember. Possibly around the same time I began to discover colors and chose red as my forever favorite. And now, after all the bad mouthing chocolate has received from the food experts, someone in the FDA has actually discovered that it might even be good for us. Turns out it's full of flavinoids and maybe a few antioxidants. Who would have thought? I must have discerning taste buds after all. We are not talking about namby pamby milk chocolate either. That stuff is for chocolate interns. We're talking about the seriously dark gastronomic delight that contains as little disturbances as possible, just enough sweetness to keep the mouth from puckering up after the flavor bursts through. And white chocolate? What was the chocolatier thinking when he came up with that? All our conscious living tells us that white chocolate is a sin against nature. Chocolate is brown; vanilla is white, and never the twain shall meet.

In a world full of important distinctions to make, chocolate falls right up there with the best of them. It is far more satisfying than getting drunk; it paves the road to hell with its delectable forms. (What child has not lusted for a chocolate Easter Bunny?) And it is almost as good as sex......almost.

All of us are called upon to do important and valuable things with our lives. Childhood lasts but a brief few years, and then we are to stand up and accept the mantle of adulthood. We shoulder many responsibilities, such as providing for the sick, voting in elections, raising the young, and making a few bucks from time to time. Who can blame us for turning to a little succor for our heavy burdens? And before us, ready to ease our troubled minds, wrapped in shining rainment, able to fill the bill, is chocolate!

On Right and Wrong

Once upon a time I knew the difference between right and wrong. Or at least I thought I did. It was right to tell the truth; it was wrong to lie. It was right to respect the feelings of others; it was wrong to be rude and disrespectful. Certainly people who were not married did not move in together, and being a Christian was the right way to worship. Then one day or maybe several days or several decades on, everything changed, and right and wrong became moveable feasts. All one has to do is watch the political scene for a while to see what a fine art lying has become. Civility often flies out the window when it comes to communicating with one another, regularly replaced by clenched fists and four-letter words. Now housewarming parties are on the rise for unwed folk who choose to live together and start families. And how more multiplied are our churches, mosques, temples and gurdwaras.

What has happened? Were we all wrong about right and wrong? Was ours just an ethnocentric point of view invented by a slice of culture but not shared by all? Who can say anymore, and perhaps the growing up process is always overtaking what we thought we knew. Perhaps we were always meant to question our foundations so that we could come to trust our own thoughts. Perhaps the questions cause us to develop personal morals on which we can really stand. Turns out that no one can know for us what we can only know for ourselves.

Over the passing years I have come to ask a different set of questions. I no longer ask whether something is right or wrong. I am not sure what the "right thing to do" is anymore, and so I frame my decisions with these questions: Does what I am about to do affirm life? Does it allow the survival of my own well being and that of the person or situation at hand? There is so much freedom in the wings of allowances. People or ideas do not have to die because they fall into someone's culture of wrongness. It is possible to stand secure on that which brings the largest dose of life and vitality at any moment. Imagine the joy that could be let loose!

I would like to think it is possible for human beings to grow up as a species, where the harsh walls of my "rightness" and your "wrongness" are dismantled, brick by brick, log by log. I would like to think, like author Emmet Fox, that there is really no wall that enough love could not throw down, and enough shared inner searching could build whole, new structures for living. Maybe the twin towers of right and wrong were only man made after all and that bridges might be better connectors.

On Toddlers

Toddlers are fabulous, some of the coolest people God ever made...and they know it. On the internet, I found a recent photo of a fierce-looking toddler with a caption saying, "A toddler's job is to rule the universe," and they seem to be very busy at it. Our great granddaughter is a two-year-old flying machine. When she comes to our home, she makes her token visit to my lap, which lasts about thirty seconds. I begin to talk of cabbages and kings, and then she snickers and hops down. Quiet stop over!

What toddlers are really good at is barreling through doorways, regardless of who may be on the other side. I think this is because they simply cannot imagine anyone's getting in their ways, so when I see a car with the caution sign in the window saying, Toddler on board, the caution is not quite complete. It should also add, Look out below!

To be sure, toddlers fuss and tantrum up now and again, but for the most part they are genuine purveyors of joy. Their inclination to smile is amazing, even at strangers. I have felt for a long time that the very young and the very old both seem to be closer to God. Maybe it's because the one is so lately come from the realms of spirit and the other so soon to return. At any rate they seem to move through their days with a lot less constriction and a lot more unregulated ease. Maybe they are not crowded as those of us in between.

Sooner or later, unfortunately, toddlers have to at least begin the process of becoming civilized, especially if they expect to survive to adulthood and head off as much mayhem as possible. Small fits and tantrums may be cute and tolerated in a small child who runs up and down the hall screeching. It is not fun when similar behaviors continue on into adulthood. At the end of the day I figure we all need as many friends as we can get, and at least a little civilization helps with this. The trick is to be able to teach some morals, manners and management without submerging a vibrant spirit under mountains of rules and regulations.

How hard would it be to carry some of the unbridled curiosity of toddlerhood with us into our grown-up years? And who said we were ever supposed to be done growing up anyway? I think that observing toddlers can give us pause to remember the preciousness of our whole lives, especially since the spontaneity of extreme youth is so brief. The toddler grows up before our very eyes, and we must be swift in gathering in how important that boundless part of us is. Otherwise how are we going to be able to burst through doorways in later life...and get away with it!

On Youth and Age

The trouble with getting older is that it is hard to remember what it was like to be young. So how can I give a perspective on youth and age? Maybe a retrospective will be as good as it gets. I do remember falling on my face as a kid and breaking a front incisor. That wasn't great, and neither was being pulled from my mother's grasp during a parade in downtown San Francisco. That was downright scary when this wall of giants pushed my mother away from me. So some parts of youth were not all that hot. Turns out, too, that with each advancing year of age I lose a year on the other end. Not helpful for trying to gather up memories. I do recall some very nice years spread in between youth and age, very nice years indeed which shall remain safely quiet in the recesses of my memory vault.

I am, however, getting really good at making assessments about growing older. Some wag once said that old age is not for sissies. He was probably right, but he might also have added that it is not for sprinters either. Somewhere along the line those lithe limbs have seized up a bit and make getting places a lot more effortful. But it is not this that I consider the enemy. Not being a natural athlete, I keep exercised enough to get the bod where I want it to go. The real enemy is wrinkles, not just one but the entire body of them. I have tried every wrinkle cream known to man, and none have made a dent in the relentless, downward march of gravity, except for the dent made in my bank account. At this point I have even considered naming some of my most defiant offenders. (I see you there, Cousin Eyefold!)

Silliness aside, I do know that the pieces of me I treasure most seem unaffected by the galloping years. I have come to trust my discernment enough to know that television really is more inane than ever, that whiter teeth doeth not a princess make, and watching a guy having a conversation with his iPhone is not funny. There are no wrinkles in my mind. In fact there are many more interesting insights to check out than ever I had imagined in my younger days. My thinking process is not suffering from arthritis, so there are no hitches in my git-along there. The smoothness of stepping from one idea to another has become much less painful, and I don't mind having to think again about something that once seemed so important. Maybe it's because, in the world of things and doings, nothing is that important anymore.

I am aware that I have a lot more physical past than future before me. Nevertheless tomorrow looks pretty good to me. Let us consider the alternative!

On Questions and Answers

Like most people, at one time when I asked questions, I was looking for answers...in nice, neat terms that closed the circle of unknowing. These days I have discovered that answers aren't all they are cracked up to be. I am often more interested in just asking the questions to see the energy that the questions generate; maybe because there don't seem to be many really durable answers, sometimes only partial or simply a path to more questions.

Some answers are completely unsatisfactory. When the grieving parent asks, "Why did my child have to die?", no simple answer will suffice. To blame God by saying that He wanted the child closer to Him is no answer at all. It only makes God the universal fall guy for difficult things that don't fall into neat categories. Some answers begin to show up only when "hard" thinking makes us look at possibilities we never wanted to see. Some questions continue to bedevil us when everyone around us knows the answers, and they know them because they don't have to be responsible for them. Would we be willing to stop asking why we can't hold a job when the answer staring us in the face is that we don't want to work? Would we be willing to stop asking why we can't keep a relationship when the answer staring us in the face is that we drink too much? Maybe it depends on when and how we ask the questions.

Some questions can be easily answered, of course. Short-term answers aren't rocket science. Why did I run out of gas? (Because, silly, you forgot to fill the tank.) Test questions all have answers. We just have to be working in the field of these answers to tease them out. Some answers are not a big deal because the questions don't mean much either. In fact they barely make a ripple in the scheme of things. "What's for dinner" doesn't take up much mental space.

Then there are the questions that are never meant to be answered, not in the finite realm at least. Or there are the questions that only have an intimate answer to the one asking the question. These are the silent questions, never given a voice. I call these soul questions that we ask within ourselves, questions that impact whatever greater sense of Self we may experience. Also there are categorical questions that involve interest in certain areas of curiosity. The spiritual seeker might ask, How can I know God, a question whose answer cannot be given by anyone external to ourselves. The apprentice mechanic asks, where does this bolt go, and the boss complies with a reply. Eventually, at the end of whatever thousands of questions we may be asking over time, there will come the big, unanswerable one...What lies ahead? Good question!

On Fear and Ignorance

When I am making points, I always try to find a solid foundation on which to stand. I do this so that I don't have to back off my intended conclusions any more than necessary. It gets downright embarrassing to find that your ideas are full of holes. This brings me to a ground I really embrace, one that I think will endure. Consider: There is only one sin, and this is ignorance. Does this seem way too simple, not complex enough? Let's look for just a moment at what ignorance breeds. Some things come to mind immediately...mistrust, hatred, war-like behaviors, exclusionary tactics, the unwillingness to learn. Important scatterings, yes, but the biggest scion of ignorance is fear, for I believe that all anti-social agendas and behaviors are fear based. All other negatives are just its offshoots.

Ignorance of those people or things that are different than ourselves cause us to fear them, and if we fear, we suspect, and suspicion is only one glance away from hatred and exclusion. The largest institution in 16th Century Europe was the Catholic

Church, which held considerable dominion over the lives of believers. When the scientist, Galileo, espoused the Copernican system of the heliocentric universe, the church considered his work as heresy and confined him to his home for the final eight years of his life. Does this sort of ignorance and fear seem unthinkable today? Perhaps, but some of our current behaviors toward others don't refute this. The ongoing strife between Israel and the Palestinians tell us otherwise. In his talks with leaders of both sides, I remember President Clinton's admonition to put aside the "easy habits of hatred" for the "hard task of reconciliation." Obviously this hard task has not been accomplished.

In our own lives, do we have easy habits that we have fallen into? This would not be difficult. Few of us are taught to hold complete equanimity toward our brothers and sisters in life. Even though I have spent many years as a minister, I have come to believe that religions create far more harm than good. Most perpetuate exclusionary behaviors. We have seen fundamentalists of all beliefs kill the stranger in the name of their God and believe themselves justified in doing so.

Where do ignorance and fear lie? Where are their shrines to be found? In the human heart, I would suggest. Writers and speakers project no real meanings unless they impress the reader or listener with the desire to act. Latent thoughts remain in the recesses of the mind until people give them footprints on the ground. Of course we, the thinkers, get to choose what thoughts we will act upon. If we want it, there is an antidote to ignorance and fear, and this would certainly seem to be learning and love. The good news is that ignorance is not a terminal condition; stupidity is. And ignorance can be cured through big doses of Einstein's "holy curiosity." What if we as a species decided to extend our curiosity a bit farther and opened our hearts a bit more. Would it be possible that we could change the world?

On Choosing to Love

We may come into life with a natural gift of love, but we have to learn how to access it, and we must choose to use it. I'm not just talking about the call of the organs to each other or sloppy-mouth love, although these are in the mix. I'm thinking of what the philosopher, Ernest Holmes, called "the grandest healing and drawing power on earth," perhaps the single most important quality of life we possess. Psychiatrist, Gerald Jampolsky, wrote of love as the only thing that is eternal and that everything else is transitory. This is very big stuff, indeed, giving what seems like a sometimes fleeting experience so much importance in our lives. But consider the alternative. What would our lives be like if we only acted from fear, anger, vengefulness or self loathing? What if we bypassed love altogether and simply let the winds of circumstances blow us about?

When we choose to love, we take our lives into our own hands. When we choose to love, we are deciding that we are worthwhile enough to make the effort—and so is what we choose to love. Love really has healing in its wings. People who love live vital lives, and no one ever overlooks them, even if they are not prominent in the public eye. When we are in the company of people who love, we just feel better. By now it is common knowledge that infants who are not cuddled or paid attention to do not thrive. This should be obvious; the tiny person who is not yet capable of sorting out complex emotions only is aware of the lightness of love or the darkness of its absence.

Love is not complicated, but we make it so. Love enhances life; love shines, that is, when it is not occluded by distractions thrown in its way. Love is strong, but it can be derailed by misunderstanding. My favorite definition of love is one given by Ernest Holmes: "Love is the self-givingness of the Spirit through the desire of life to express itself in terms of creation." Think of it! Love fired by God! What if Holmes is right? What would this make us? God-lings? God-lets? Human beings with an essential, spiritual nature? Sounds good to me, but it also brings us a dilemma that we will wrestle with every day of our lives. If we are made of love's desire for expression, how do we work with this in a world that seems so often unloving? At least we are better at recognizing love—or at least love in action—when we see it...people caring, people helping, people coming together. Just as we know when it is not in action...people hating, people killing, people destroying. Love may always be present but sometimes its light is out.

We are back to choice again, and I think what is really important is knowing that what others may be doing has nothing to do with us. We do not have to give love to get love. If we exist because of the burst of love's creative energy, how can we ever be outside it? We belong to it, whether or not people love us in the ways we would like. Our choices are freely ours, dependent on nothing and no one outside ourselves. Whether it is difficult or easy makes no difference at all. We can build a fence—or we can build a bridge. Choice again.

On Life

We do care about life, not just our own, but the furtherance of life in general. Why else would there be a strip of marine parks along the coast from Mexico to Oregon? Why else did the American president, Teddy Roosevelt, begin the establishment of the American National Parks System in the early years of the 20th Century? And why else would people give time and energy to protecting thousand-year-old redwoods in the Pacific Northwest? Even in our egocentricity we understand that the lives of animals, whose voices we are just beginning to understand, are as important as our own.

If we are thinking at all about what lives need to thrive, let alone simply function, we should also be thinking about how rapidly we are consuming the means to thrive. It is rather amazing to think that a self-generative planet like earth could ever run out of resources, but apparently it can. Who would have thought that water was a one-time gift and not something that infinitely pours from the heavens for our use? We now know that it simply recycles itself in a rather small, circular fashion. Left to its own devices the water cycle would flush and cleanse itself regularly, but it is no longer left to its own devices, of course. The human faction is now intrusive enough to invade the self-generating systems of the earth, probably because it has no voice to tell its human inhabitants what they are doing.

How many of us in the bygone days of industrialization and the current days of technology ever thought of the earth as anything other than a resource to be plundered? Early in the Genesis story man was given dominion over the earth. Too bad the term wasn't construed as partnership, for then our view of our planet might have been different early on. Native people have intuitively known that their lives were inextricably bound to the health of their surroundings. As the land and its animal inhabitants were secure, so were their own lives. All modern communities need to do is read the histories of the Plains Indians to see what thoughtless sport shooting of buffalo did to the well being of those who depended on them for their food and supplies.

We're back where we started, once more caring about life but with our eyes open. We now know that we are all in this life together, and that ultimately we must all thrive, or none will thrive. Our interconnection is now unmistakable. Certainly our troubled, global banking systems tell us that there are no boundaries to crisis. Apparently some people are hunkering down and getting closer to their vital roots, especially since most ordinary people feel helpless to affect the global watchers. Young people even want to use open land to grow food. Could we become citizens again rather than just consumers, giving back and not just taking? Guess it depends upon how much life, including our own, matters.

On Oneness

Oneness is such a clunky word. It does not imitate a grand sweep of thought suggested by a word like in-ter-con-nec-tion. Such a word takes time to trip off the tongue. A word like this tends to make the mind soar over the landscapes of thought like a plane taking in vistas of ground going on past what the eye can see. Still, a word like connection implies something like disconnection as its alter ego. What can be joined together can be separated. A weld can be broken apart. Our clunky Oneness, on the other hand, implies only no otherness, and in Oneness everything else is allowed...form, void, ugliness, beauty, harmony, even discord. Can discord be included in Oneness? Does the roundness, square-ness, infinitesimalness, unimaginableness and grandness of Oneness dictate that conflict is not included? Well, if it can't be, we're in big trouble. If hard things are not a part of Oneness, we have no imagination about Oneness at all. We'll keep blowing off feel-ings of hatefulness, vengefulness, war, murder and mayhem of all sorts, thinking these could not possibly be a part of something as pristine as Oneness. If these dark experiences are not found in the folds of Oneness, where are they found? Where are they lodged?

Certainly not in a non-existent "otherness." Where, then, but in our capacities for misunderstanding Oneness altogether.

Therein lies the concern... the misunderstanding of Oneness altogether. There should be no surprises in this. In the realms of physical forms and experiences where egos dance, it is very easy to create myths about more and less, worthiness and unworthiness, beautiful and ugly. In our fear and suspicion of one another we do not notice our ultimate kinship. Our eyes are blind to it, and so we create imaginary gulfs that can lead to the worst misunderstanding of all: My way is better than yours, and therefore I am better than you. But this thinking leads only to the killing of bodies, not an imagined prevalence of good over evil or right over wrong.

If we were to winnow down our theories and prognostications about Oneness, we would discover that there really is only dumb Oneness or smart Oneness, something that is always on hand and shifting one way or the other anyway. When I eye you with fear or distrust I am dumb in my Oneness. When I recognize our essential spiritual natures over behaviors and beliefs, skin color or geography, when I recognize the "skin-deepness" of my own perceptions, I am beginning to get smart. Reason and intuition would inform me regularly and keep me sweet tempered if I but let them. Eventually at the end of the day, smart Oneness tells me that the sharp-edged distinctions aren't durable. They come and go as they always have. And at the end of the end of the day, after all that I have loved or hated disappears entirely, I am left with...Oneness.

On Our Humanity

I believe that we have a deep, spiritual core within us and that it is consistently revealing itself in our human lives, which is the only place it can be played out. The only way we can be really known by others is in the way we live our lives. This is a no-brainer. While we walk the earth we leave our footprints, and by these we will be known. It is not easy to be a loving, caring, self-aware human being. We know this because so much of our lives, mostly of necessity, are involved with using our talents and by our relationships with money and its alter ego, power. We are faced with the question: Will I have enough money to fulfill my needs? And if we are ambitious, the questions change: Will I always be able to do what I want to do? Will I have more money than my family and friends?

If money becomes important in how we define ourselves, it will not be difficult to begin to equate our well being with "How much can I buy?" And this gives money a whole different focus...and a whole lot more power. Author, Michael Sandel, has been assessing the role of the market place in the world economy but particularly in American life. He has written that "we drifted from having a market economy to being a market society." If he is right, we are coming close to a time when we must morally ask: Is there anything that money can't buy? If this question seems outrageous, let us remember that, in today's world, we can buy children through the adoptive and surrogacy processes. Those with enough money can buy small islands from sovereign governments, and through the use of an unlimited flood of money, elections will be up for grabs, essentially bought and sold. As living, breathing, loving, thinking, choosing, deciding individuals I think that if the values we hold dear become influenced by money, our humanity will be in great danger of eroding. We will be in danger of seeing greater inequality in life because those without much money will never get to the head of the line anymore. Someone will have bought their places. And, as Sandel suggests, the things and qualities that mean so much to us as human beings will become corrupted...not necessarily because they are dealt with illegally but because their true values will be cheapened. They will just be commodities, up for negotiation. They will not be sacred or inviolable anymore; they will just be purchase-able.

I believe that there will always be a place in us that will need to think through what the world is throwing at us. Is the seductive world of getting and having sucking the brains and morals right out of us? Is genuine contemplation vanishing from the scene? Harsh thinking? Perhaps. But we are still individuals that know how to ask: Does this seem right? Is there any holiness in this deal, and what might be the unintended consequences? We can still say yes…and no!

On Ordinary People

Are there times when the great, the wise and the wonderful, as well as the down and dismayed, become just ordinary people? I believe there are. I believe there are enough equalizers in life to remind us that we are all answerable to the things of the earth and the heavens. When the believer goes on the Hajj to Mecca, he becomes like all the others circling the Kaaba. He takes off his finery or his tattered clothing and dons simple, white garments, so that he may be reminded that all are equal to God. Women wear the simple hijab. None stand out to be distinguished above their brothers and sisters.

To me, a day at the park fills this bill perfectly well. We can enjoy our ordinariness in all its glory. People are biking, jogging, roller blading, flying kites, walking dogs, and sitting on the grass to their hearts' content. Even the visiting, red-tailed hawk with his splendid plumage is humbled by noisy, antagonistic crows...the panoply of the commonplace on parade in all its unassuming holiness. Stranger can still greet stranger in the outdoor commons with a smile, a few words or a shared spectacle of nature in its uncensored offerings, and none of it is done hesitantly or fearfully.

It is really too bad that we must leave these even playing fields to return to what is expected of us. The potentate will resume his robes and duties when he returns from the Hajj; the business person will put on his or her office togs. Even the person whose limited mobility feels easier and sunnier in the park will return once more to his cramped surroundings. The good thing is that these days and times wait for us. The park is there; the walking trails never close, and the breezes kick up regularly for the kite flyers. If we frequent the park enough, we get to know some of the regulars. In my park there is a man I call the "kite guy" who puts up several, enormous, flamboyant kites most weekends. They catch the winds and light the sky with their twists, twirls and outrageous colors. Who cannot stop to watch this engaging show, given all for nothing?

There is something absolutely redemptive in knowing that there are endless opportunities for us to enjoy the uncomplicated parts of ourselves...not painted over or specially garbed, and that they can be shared—or not—with other uncomplicated folks in an ordinary state. When we can look into the sky or feel our footprints on the ground, all naturally directed, it is as if we belong to ourselves again. And there is nothing and no one to answer to but our own thoughts.

On Death

Unless one is raised in a culture where death has a daily presence, I don't think most people give it a second thought, especially the young. They are, of course, still immortal, and that doesn't change much unless they are suddenly slammed with the unexpected death of a peer. Afterward they gather themselves together, and their natural focus on life takes over once more. I was one of those kids, just cooking along with no intrusions, no deaths of school mates. Never thought much about much more than growing up, dating, getting married, many of the things one does into young adulthood. One day that all changed because of one vital man.

My husband and I were friends with an older man who was hale, energetic, foxy and highly interested in younger people. He was fascinated by their thoughts and interests and was constantly asking questions about their decisions. When he was talking to you, he would focus all the attention of his sparkling blue eyes and considerable wit upon you, and you were very aware of his interest in you. Then suddenly he began to get sick with an aggressive cancer, which took his life in a very short time. And there we were, seeing his composed flesh for the last time laid out in one of his signature, three-piece suits. His body was not savaged by the illness, and so he seemed almost asleep. One might have expected him to open his eyes at any moment, except for one thing...the twinkle was gone, absolutely gone. This was a man who radiated life from his very pores, and now it was completely absent. In that instant I began a many-year trek into the valley of death.

Certainly I had basic beliefs about the continuity of life, beliefs I espouse to this day, but death had not been a part of this equation until the loss of a twinkle forced me to think about it. Perhaps I took life so for granted that I took death for granted too. I was so busy living that I never realized I was also busy dying. I found that most people did not want to talk about dying, maybe because they feared that talking about it might bring it closer to the front door, like an uninvited guest who wanted to use the second bedroom. I used to think that life and death had no relationship and that they were irrevocably separated. After conducting many funerals and memorials with families, I now believe that they belong together, that they are just two ends of the same stick.

Doesn't it seem obvious that our lives move in a seamless flow of beginnings and endings, many series of miniscule births and deaths and that as one cycle ends, another begins? Nature knows this and does not fight the passing of the seasons. Why should I? As I grow older and celebrate the births of new babies and adventures in new businesses, I can look out of the corner of my eye and see the Reaper winking at me. I'm not afraid; I'm curious, mostly about what form the newest twinkle will take.

On Hanging On

Outside my front door I keep two hanging baskets of fuchsias. Everyone likes them, visitors, hummingbirds, robber birds in search of nesting material. Certainly my husband and I do as we enjoy seeing them outside our kitchen window as we have breakfast. They bloom every minute they are alive. They never run out of steam, and they continuously drop flowers on the patio floor below. If I wanted to, I could sweep up flowers every day, so many are always falling. Sometimes my thoughts get a little convoluted as I try to fit some of life's living pieces together, and so I found myself wondering about the profligacy of the fuchsias. Why are they wasting all that flower power, I thought. Why don't they save a little energy by hanging on a little longer? Why aren't they more like roses that hang on until you have to cut them off? But then, of course, fuchsias are not roses and who knows how fuchsia brains work! Obviously they are smart enough to know that, when they let old blossoms fall, there is plenty of room for new ones to come forth.

There is an obvious metaphor here. Human beings know a whole lot about hanging on. In fact we are usually so good at it that we often don't recognize when a thing is dead and hang on to it long past the time when it begins to stink, be it a dead fish, a sack of garbage or a relationship. In the world of relationships there is always the possibility of cutting out too soon before the bud begins to blossom, but this is usually done when people don't understand the need for time in for development. Mostly it's just hanging on too long—when the parties involved have left the situation mentally, if not physically, or when people are too afraid that they won't blossom again

We sometimes hang on to our very lives when change looms before us. I have been privileged to have spent many hours with people as the end of their physical lives approached. In years past when people did not understand the connection between life and the doorway called death, they clung to life desperately, fearing what they could not imagine. These years many of us have come to think about the connective cycles of life, and so we have less need to hang on to a finished experience and more willingness to imagine what might lie ahead. I have seen brave folks close the book on a body that was used up and set their sights on what was newer. This only happens when we are willing to let go of what was known and embrace what is unknown. Good thing we're able learners and maybe carry a little of the fuchsia mind in us.

On Stuff

I think that most George Carlin lovers are aware of his nefar-
iously funny monologue on "stuff." One thing that made the
late comedian's style so humorous was his gift of poking fun
at many revered and iconic beliefs and practices. He could not
wait to tease anything (or anyone) that he thought was being
taken too seriously by the public...or sometimes by important
people themselves. His take on stuff was a jab at us for taking our accumulations with such fervor and vigor. What made
this monologue so memorable was because it hit us all in our
acquisitive hearts. We do love our stuff, and isn't that's what
money is for...to get more stuff?

Let's get serious for a moment. What is stuff anyway? Did
you know what a big deal stuff is? There is a definition of
stuff in the dictionary that takes up a whole lot of space, more
than Argentina or archeology, and you'd think they would
be more important than stuff! Looks like stuff is a whole lot
more complicated than it seems. The dictionary has many def-
initions of it, such as: the material of which everything is to
be made, or just simply...things. This is no help. We already

know that stuff is things and that stuff is made up of material or...other stuff.

Looks like we're going to have to take things (make that, stuff) in hand and give stuff some real study. Now there are some things that we obviously already know about stuff. There is big stuff and little stuff, expensive stuff and cheap stuff, beautiful stuff and ugly stuff, and maybe most important of all...stuff we could never, ever think of getting rid of. Think of it! Who would we be without our stuff? Imagine not having any stuff to wear or eat! And what if we could not borrow our sister's stuff or leave our stuff in our dad's garage...next to his stuff!

And another thing. Is all stuff visible? Does it always fill drawers and corners and closets everywhere? Or does stuff also take up room in our minds? I know of myself that my mind can get so full of stuff that I can barely think. At night sometimes there is so much stuff to think about that I can hardly get to sleep. And if sometimes I should happen to have a nice, quiet space in my mind where nothing much is going on, I can always bring up stuff! I can bring up old memories, old problems, old hurts—really miserable stuff—and be right at home with my old stuff once again. Come to think of it, all this talk about stuff is making me really depressed. Wherever he is I hope Carlin knows how much terror he has stricken in the hearts of those of us who must have our stuff!

On A Fine Obsession

When the Olympic Games are due we, the viewing public are, of course, made aware that they are coming. We get sound bytes showing us the graceful athletes at work in their fields, and sometimes we can watch hopeful children doing handsprings in the living room. We are treated to shots of parents waking kids in the wee hours so that they can take them to practices before school starts. These are tender, admirable scenes, and they depict what I call a fine obsession, which is what it takes to create a prize-winning athlete. We all know that those racks of muscles don't come with a few push-ups. All the skills, muscles and fortitude come with years of consistent practice, and it is the same with any other fine development of arts or scientific studies.

These are the fine obsessions that create prize winners, and this is the aim—to win the medal, the scholarship, the contract, the trophy. But what separates the winners from the others—one one hundredth of a second, the right prevailing winds, a chrystalline high C? And what of the "others"? Are they somehow less skilled, less magnificent, less outstanding than they were before they became an other? And what of being judged a winner, which is an imperfect art in itself? Some judgments are highly subjective, as we know, and some, as we also know, are corrupted through bribes and special deals. Within the whole arena of competitions, so much confusion and obstruction have built up that a prize is not simply a prize and a loss not just a loss. Winning can mean status, money and fame for at least a while; losing can mean disgrace. I am reminded that at one Olympic Games Chinese athletes who did not win went home despised. Can you give your all to some competitive challenge for years and then suddenly withdraw it or at least mitigate it when the drive is no longer there?

Not being one of the finely obsessed, I would hope that winning a recognizable goal is not all that the long hours and practices are for. I would hope that a great amount of becoming is the more certain prize. In living our lives we come to know that there are things, knowings and givings that no one can do for us. No book, no teacher, and no coach can bring this magic to us. Love can act as encouragement. Time into working with our obsessions can turn a base metal into real gold, which is a special alchemy indeed. At the end of the day the finely-tuned soul could ask what are the meanings of winning and losing. What prizes do the rich turnings of a life hold when all the gains and losses are gathered in? The fine obsession can teach us this.

On Fathers

Here's to fathers, to those who waited anxiously while we were being born, to those who indulged in some distant fling and didn't even know they were fathers. Here's to them all anyway. Whether or not they were good and thoughtful parents, they made it possible for us to come into life, and for that alone they deserve some credit. I've known a few dads, my own specifically, and the one who made it possible for me to become a mother. On the whole I'd say they were a pretty good lot.

Taking trips back into memory lane is always a tricky business. For some reason we tend to go back to sad or hard memories. This does not prove helpful. If we're thinking about deficient dads, sitting on old, bad memories will not do anything but make a difficult time worse—and new all over again when it deserves to be left in the halls of memory. If we're looking into a dad's casket, good memories may suddenly pop up in a flood of nostalgia. Nice, but a little late. Should have done that one sooner.

My father has been dead for many decades, and he lived at a time when people, including doctors did not believe in bringing up serious illness to a dying patient. During my father's last illness, we all knew he was dying, but ostensibly he did not—unless he was fooling us and knew at some inner level. He never said so. The loaded silence among us did not allow us to talk with him, to ask him what he was thinking and feeling or if he was afraid. We could not cry together or comfort one another. We could only wait until his heart suddenly stopped and he just ceased breathing. In those days we didn't know any better. Hopefully we have grown up some since then. Maybe we've come to know that some things are better said than unsaid. Dads can't read our minds, and if there are important things to say, we had better do so. If we have older fathers around, they need to know what we are thinking so that they still have opportunities to continue being the best dads ever or make a good effort at being a better one. If we have young dads among us, it is foolishness to assume they will all live to be old dads. Some don't, and many exchanges of love can be lost in waiting just a little too long to let them know how important they are. My father had very little education, but he took his family responsibilities very seriously. There was a lot of art in him, and he made beautiful, finely-etched jewelry—for his girls, my mother and me. My father-in-law, another good dad, was a first-generation immigrant to the United States. Not well educated either and always struggling with the language, he could build just about anything, which I later learned was a very European trait. I had a brief but lovely opportunity to have a step father. A dear and graceful man gave my mother's later life great sweetness, but unfortunately, only for a bare few years. He had no children of his own but he could not have loved my mother's children more. And let me not forget the two sons who grew up to be fine fathers themselves...and are still at it.

On the whole...a pretty good lot.

On Mothers

One thing I know about motherhood—it never ends. Those sweet little children may have gray hair now; they are still our kids. They may have more money than we, or maybe a whole lot less; they're still our kids. Or sadly, some of those smiling youngsters may be in prison for serious crimes, serious enough that we may be unable to see them for long periods of time, but they're still our kids. As mothers we know that our children come through us and that they don't belong to us, but there is a reckless unreasoning in us that still feels the connection to them, though they may have long escaped from our bodies. I sometimes think motherhood is not so much a biological condition as a state of mind. Perhaps this is why women who may never have physically borne children can still make fine mothers.

Mothers are built for the long haul. They may be blessed in having a terrific husband and father on hand, but even if they don't, if they are reasonable and healthy, they are in it to the finish. I don't think that some will consider motherhood a job, something that is an add-on to our lives. Babies change everything. Even someone who becomes a mother unintentionally becomes highly involved with the tiny person in her care. She may be unsure, even frightened at the thought of such responsibility, but she learns and she accepts. I think a nursing mother feels an almost mystical tie with the child at her breast, knowing that for a brief while the babe is entirely dependent on her flowing substance for its life. I know I felt that way, and I think it's this tie that turns the hapless young woman into a raging tigress if her child seems threatened.

Good mothers carry healing in their bones...and in their spit! When I was a child, if I fell and scratched myself, my mother simply took a little saliva from her tongue and swiped it on the small abrasion. "There, all better." Somehow, it worked, even though today we know that this was a highly unsanitary thing to do. Mothers do unusual things at times. I saw a whimsical commercial that featured a mother performing all sorts of outrageous acts to keep her son from harm—jumping over fences, standing in front of him in a basketball game so that another player could not thump him. It was funny and outlandish, yes, but not really removed from a mother's mind. The creator of the commercial quite understood the button that causes a mother to act, almost without thinking. Maybe it was another mother.

Mothers work from the heart of forgiveness more than anyone I know. Time and time again things do not turn out the way they would like, and people disappoint, perhaps even a beloved child. They know the meaning of second chances and are willing to give them, and maybe thirds and fourths or fifths. When the Master, Jesus, was asked how often one should forgive, he replied, "Seventy times seven," which implies continual forgiveness.

Perhaps he was thinking of mothers.

On Parenthood

I think that good parenting is always a choice. Babies may be the offspring of a biological urge, but parenting them is quite another matter. We do not come into life with natural skills for this, and we do not learn them all by ourselves. We are taught them by people who have been parents before us, our own or others who have stood in the place of parents to us. I think there is true genius in good parenthood and real devastation when it is poor, and part of that devastation comes when we learn that the price of poor parenting is not borne by us but by our unfortunate children. It takes real devotion to train a child to become a genuine, real-time adult, someone who is capable of self control, yet able to catch an unexpected star of creativity and act on it. I believe that when good parenting is not on hand, children do not grow up to be real adults; they just grow larger, more muscular, hairy bodies containing minds that never outgrew adolescence.

We could ask another, very pertinent question: Is there only one honorable combination of parents? Must the combination be only male and female? Actually not, as it turns out. We might ask instead what the working, pragmatic qualities of good parenthood are rather than the gender make up. Biology alone does not guarantee good parenthood, which is self evident. I have always thought it interesting that it takes the proper licenses to sell apples on the street, but any reproducing pair can have a child at any time anywhere. With all our new technologies and growing awarenesses, could we not get a better handle on this? Does freedom mean that evolving humanity continue to reproduce indiscriminately without a second thought?

And of the children who are with us, would they be better off with two unhealthy, male-female parents than with two of the same sex who have had to prepare themselves for what's at stake? It is important to remember that parenting is a learned skill, and we don't get many second chances. I guess I would also ask: Can children have too many people loving them? Blended families find a place in my thoughts here, especially if birth parents and step parents understand that children really need to be loved with intelligence and inspiration rather than be fought over and used as leverage.

Good parenting involves a subtle knowledge of the differences between never enough and too much. I think that there can never be enough love for children, but there can be too much granted wish fulfillment and anticipated entitlement, especially when the family adults will not say no when necessary. Since all children grow up one way or another, I guess the last question I would ask might be: Did I love wisely?

On Hummingbirds

I heard a naturalist once say that he thought hummingbirds had the personality of a junkyard dog, and, boy, was he right. Our front yard allows for a lot of trafficking by hummers, and they are, without doubt, some of the meanest of all nature's creatures. For their tiny size, they are amazingly combative. If I happen to go out the front door while they are feeding, they will buzz me as if to say, "Hey, you're in my way!" They seem absolutely unconcerned about the fact that my husband and I, the disruptive householders, are the ones who keep their feeders full. Talk about buzzing the head that feeds you! And they are certainly no better to each other. I have no idea whether or not I am watching males or females; they all seem equally miserable. We keep the two feeders filled, and there is an abundance of hummers' favorite blossoms right by them; nevertheless the tiny marauders chase off any others who invade their territory. You'd think there would be plenty of food opportunities to go around, yet they seem afraid of some possible lack, much like many human beings. Occasionally one hummingbird will perch on a branch inside a nearby bush, just waiting for an unsuspecting thief to trespass his space. I actually watched one little guy sit for twenty minutes guarding his turf before he flew off, something I never thought possible.

In all my years of hummer watching I was on hand for an amazing sight once and only once. One early evening a sudden and heavy rain occurred, quiet unexpectedly. As always our four-positioned feeder was full when suddenly four hummers took all the positions and fed, with a fifth hovering in wait. And not one drove off the others! Unthinkable! What could the little bird brains have been thinking? Were there too few blossoms available in other places that year? Were they just too hungry to care? What it did suggest was that even old birds can learn new tricks!

During my fascination with these flashing natural helicopters, I have become aware once more of the essential connections we share with living things. These days when I go out the front door, they seem somehow a little "nicer" to me, if that's the word. They patiently let me pass unbuzzed. Perhaps they have come to recognize the food bringer at last. Perhaps I just now have been allowed in their scenes. A friend once told me a fabulous story about hummer behavior. He was watering his yard one day when a hummingbird suddenly flew into the fine spray of his hose and lingered within the droplets for several seconds. Then it flew up to him and hovered about one foot from his face, staying there a few more seconds. He told me it was if it were saying, "I know you." Perhaps if we are all still enough and issue silent invitations indiscriminately, we can recognize the connections we share, as our feathered charmer did.

On Space

Americans seem to love their space. I noticed this particularly when I was visiting in India several years ago. Whenever our group was traveling a main thoroughfare in New Delhi, I craned my neck to look into the side streets, often unpaved. There the mass of Indian humanity seemed to converge, and the streets always looked as if a baseball game had just let out and everyone was headed for their parked cars. Only those streets weren't dealing with parked cars; they were full of anything and everything that could move—pedestrians, trucks, tiny mopeds, bicycles, animals carrying cargo, and oxen unfettered by any restraints. Somehow all managed to serpentine together without any crashes, all perfectly ordinary, all in a day's activity. And only a whisper of space separating them all. It seemed the most natural choreography in the world. In a city with vast numbers, how could it be otherwise?

I could not have imagined myself moving so effortlessly with such a teeming crowd. I would have felt myself in other peoples' space, and they certainly would have been in mine. At times it was only the metal barrier that our vehicle provided that kept us from spilling over into one anothers' laps. I did not feel claustrophobic; I am not normally so afflicted. But I certainly felt crowded. Only when in our rooms or meeting places did I feel I could take a full breath without snatching someone else's air.

I like my space. I like the opportunity of being able to stand apart so that I can observe without participating, and you need space for this; otherwise you are caught in the activity that physical closeness brings. I like this too. I like the shared vitality that erupts whenever people are flooding space with their energy. I want it both ways; I want both space and closeness, and with some care and attention I can have both if I am paying heed to the signals I send out. I know when my physical person sends a message to stay away, and when I am beckoning, come. What is tricky is not sending mixed signals. I have often felt that I am a private person in a public profession and have had to learn not to intrude my private space into my public world, sometimes a delicate maneuver. There is a gift in being one of those who must manage both private and public space. I can sense when another is having difficulty in harmonizing this balance, and sometimes I can bring my quiet physical person into a place where those sharing it can take stock of where they are and what adjustments they want to make. These hard-won awarenesses are worth the effort. In an often brittle and demanding world, it is good to be able to bring a nexus into a space that needs both clarity and diffusion.

56

On Pie and Ice Cream for Breakfast

In my little piece of the American culture I was taught that you eat certain foods at certain times of the day. Consequently at breakfast we ate cereal, orange juice, eggs, etc., and so on during the day. Lunch was fruit and sandwiches, and dinner held more elaborate foods...and desserts. I was raised that way, and I raised my family that way, never really thinking about these habits much. They had become comfortably established subjective patterns in my mind.

Then a year or so ago as my husband and I were going to have breakfast with some friends, I passed the bakery counter of our restaurant of choice, and there sat a big, sumptuous apple pie—my favorite. Sudden I got a wild (to me) idea! I can have pie for breakfast and ice cream too, and the cosmos will not disintegrate! And my next thought was why in the world it took me so long to veer off the old, beaten path. I had pie and ice cream for breakfast that very day and enjoyed it thoroughly, and whenever I get a jones for it,

I have it again. As far as I can see, it hasn't shortened my life one little bit.

We are strange and interesting people. We get used to doing things in a certain way and never give them a second thought until something derails the train. Hopefully the dislocation is minor, something that causes us to take another look at how and why we do things, but often it is not simple. Often we are jarred by a sudden illness or an unexpected loss, and then we are sent scrambling. Pie and ice cream for breakfast is certainly not life changing, but what of occurrences that are? What if a scary message comes our way or something we counted on turns out not to last forever? These are the things that either drive us into our inner resources or cause us to abdicate our power altogether. As I think about these possibilities, I opt for the former. I would like to think of myself as being able to trust what I know about myself rather than give over my fate to others.

All of this means that I am going to have to cultivate more of a pie and ice cream, experimental frame of mind and be willing to unsettle my known boundaries. I can learn to dodge and weave a little bit more so that I can handle the punches life can throw. I'm not being heroic in this, maybe just a little more attentive to what I usually take for granted. I could take thought a little more rather than just drifting through the days without notice.

Funny...and breakfast used to be such a simple thing!

On Being a Mother-in-law

At times I actually think I am a better mother-in-law than I am a mother. Don't mistake me. None are closer to my heart than my children, but I know that I always have my nose in their lives way more than I should...still directing traffic, I suppose. With my in-law children, they did not start out as children to me. I always knew them as singular adults who have either married a child of mine or partnered with one. They are all unique, with their own classic characteristics and tweaks, but probably most of all, these fine adults have never become the amorphous faces referred to as "my son's wife" or "my daughter's husband." Having been so labeled as a daughter-in-law years ago, I promised myself never to do that to a promising, grown-up person...and I never have.

Long ago I gave up the myth that I could choose the "right" mates for my family members. I figured we would all grow together as contributors to a family community, and for the most part, we have. As a wise friend once said, "all of us know more than any of us," and that clever little statement has turned out to be pretty accurate. We have lost a few through divorce, but in the cases where we formed a true bond, those former in-laws have still remained family members. Perhaps it really is true that it is love and not blood that binds us together.

I think that because my in-laws are a step farther from me than my children, I can view them with more equanimity. I don't set up expectations that they must fill, and I cannot see them as extensions of myself, which is a curse I try not to lay upon my flesh and blood. In a way I guess I would say that being an in-law parent makes me a better natural parent. I hope so. At least I hope that I can hold the smaller family units as entities in themselves, which can only enhance me by their private expansions. God knows I don't need other sets of babies to rear, but I am pleased to assist when a little elder wisdom is called on. Actually the children of my children are themselves not children any more, and one of them has set off the whole, lovely cycle again with her own toddler on premises.

Now I am two steps away from being able to intrude very much, which is as it should be. Perhaps when new sets of in-laws start showing up again, we will all remember to cut them some slack. They will certainly add a new element to the gene pool and make us all a little bit more interesting than we were.

On Being the Salt of the Earth

I have a beautiful child who is the salt of the earth. She is the mustard seed fully grown into a leafy bush, sheltering all within the shade of her branches. She is the one who does what needs to be done without complaint or second thoughts...little tasks that often go unheralded, large tasks as a simple matter of course. She is herself a world of creativity, and yet she provides a gantry that lets others fly from her into their own destinies. Not wasting time on unnecessaries, she is a respite, a still point in her world, a place where others may come for a quiet reprieve from the blowing winds of their life's demands.

I have known a scattered number of such salts throughout my life, altogether too few to suit me. I have also known a great number of rocket-launching types, people who are full of lights and shadows, moving through life with flair and fol-de-rol. They create huge interest wherever they go and can be wildly entertaining. Whenever they are in the room, they cannot go

unnoticed. Still, when I am in need of unquestioning acceptance, I do not wander to these vigorous folks. I make my way
to one of my salts. They are in the room also, perhaps quietly
navigating the corners as observers, very much like an invisible calm that keeps the place from erupting completely.

It cannot be said that they are never upset. In their humanity they of course get off balance and quip or grouse. But they
always seem to have a finger on their own inner awarenesses.
They know themselves; they simply do, and so their forgetful-
ness is short lived, and they are not long out of sorts...fortu-
nately for the rest of us. If I were to be envious of any group of
people, it would be the salts of the earth, as if they were God's
own, put on earth to keep the world spinning on course while
some are defying gravity. If I could, I would lavish treasures
at their feet for what they do and who they are. I would thank
them every day for their always-given gifts. I don't very often,
though, because I know they would feel abashed, maybe a little surprised and might even wonder if I'm becoming slightly
addled. There is no overlooking these salts or being unaware of
their presences and abiding passion for living. Just let one die,
and it is as if a great chasm in the ground opens beneath our
feet, never to be filled again in the same way.

We miss them forever and never cease to look around for
them.

On Necks

Ever wonder why the words, neck and nexus, sound so much alike? It's because they mean the same thing. They are links, connections. Obviously the neck connects the head with the rest of the body. Otherwise our heads would have to be screwed on to our shoulders, and this would immediately make us shorter, which would be a problem for the already vertically challenged. We do not need to be shorter than we already are, thank you!

Some people are really into necks. I know a woman who once said she loved looking at a young man's neck, whether to bite or to kiss, she never said, and I thought it better not to ask. If we think about it, necks can be fascinating things and can raise some very interesting questions. For instance, if we did not have necks, would we get sore throats? If we did not, this could make necklessness a good thing. On the other hand we could never know what it means to have a swan-like neck, and this would be tragic for the esthetically inclined.

Think of what we might be missing if we did not have necks! How would we know what it means to be neck-and-neck? Without necks there would be no sticking out of them, nothing to be up to in them, which sounds a lot like we'd have to be contortionists. Without necks why would we ever make scary, vampire movies? Imagine! A whole genre of really weird film making and a source of great nightmares would be missing for us. Without necks we would not be able to look sideways, which certainly wouldn't help our driving skills any.

There is, however, at least one very good reason not to have necks. Guillotines would never have been invented, and Marie Antoinette would have kept her head (along with a lot of other folks.)

On the whole, I think that necks are generally a good deal. Where else would we wear a diamond choker, and don't we need a place around which to hang our medals? As I consider this heady anatomical subject, I think my favorite reason for having necks is that they allow us to look up, not just at the sky but to a much larger view of ourselves. If we were trapped at ground level, only looking straight ahead, heights and flights would be lost to us, and this loss would be inestimable.

Without doubt, necks are cool, especially for wearers of turtle-neck sweaters and long earrings.

On Distillations

To distill is to massage out all that is not wanted or needed from whatever we happen to be doing. Obviously this procedure can take us very far afield, from the world of science which continually refines its conjectures into workable theories to simple farmers in ancient fields as they toss their grain harvests on large sieves into the air, letting the wind carry away the lighter hulls from the heavier kernels. Unlike a bouillon cube which gives us a burst of concentrated flavor, distillations attenuate; they illumine the meanings of what's important...and also tend to divest the unimportant of its overdressed pretensions.

I have often said that there has to be a good reason for getting older, and I think part of this is so we can think out of perspectives instead of simply at face values. It takes time to learn that not everything is worth getting worked up over; not every piece of knowledge or experience is good to carry over into the long haul. And we are here for the long haul. It takes time and living for us to grow those lines our faces reflect over the years. To yearn for constant youth is, I think, not only a waste of time but also a terrible decision to overlook what has deepened in us through gains and losses.

I have had the pleasure of reading both the early works and the later compilations of the ontologist, Ernest Holmes. There is a distinct difference in the tenor of his early writings than those of his later considerations. The brightness and vitality of the young writings tell of a man who is enthralled with his constant discoveries, almost child-like in his enthusiastic offerings. The works of his later years indicate a man who has gathered together the foundation of an awareness on which he now rests. There is light and joy in them, yes, and there is also a more settled certainty borne of experience, practice and outcomes. His mountaintop has now become his life raft, a place of many fewer questions and more great insights...distillations, in a word. It was as if in those final years he had sifted out the scurrying and stood confidently on what he knew by extensive thinking and doing. To me, there was no mistaking the personal power of belief that he shared with the reader.

Wisdom would have us take time to pass on what has accrued to us over years of living, what has worked and what was not worth the effort, how we can learn from failures as well as successes. If we do not reveal the depths we have plumbed, the few things worth articulating, the love we have honed, there may not really be a reason for getting older after all.

On Endeavor

On September 21, 2012, the space shuttle, Endeavor, was due to make its final flight to the California Science Center in Los Angeles, California, its ultimate destination now that the United States space shuttle program has been closed down. It had one more pass to make through the California skies so that the people in that area might have the chance at a personal view of it. NASA Ames, in its kindness, waited until the San Francisco fogs had cleared so that Endeavor's flight over the spires of the Golden Gate Bridge could be seen clearly by the waiting crowd, ready with camera and videos to capture the last whisper of the U.S. shuttle program.

Our family was ready too. We knew when the shuttle was due to pass over the bridge, so we were out on our back deck which allowed us a view that was directly across from San Francisco and the bridge, and we were waiting with a sense of excitement and anticipation. Would it really be clear enough to see? Would the figures in the sky be close enough to be definitely recognizable? Suddenly there began a growing roar overhead that got loud and louder. My son, his eyes like a little boy's again, heard it first and exclaimed, "It's coming!" This, of course, drew us to look up to the sky, and there it was... Endeavor right overhead, strapped to the back of its enormous 747 carrier, majestically spearing its way through the airway. The automatic illusion that we might touch it caused us all to raise our hands in the air. The plane was flying slowly on purpose so that we might see every detail of our space traveler and its transport. Our surprise was complete; we did not know it was due to make a pass over the east bay before it arched over Marin County and gracefully soared over the bridge towers, finally moving out of view on its southward journey.

I was trembling. The experience proved transformative for me, partly because I had never imagined I would have such a treasured, close up, and partly because I knew I was involved in a once-in-a-lifetime experience. It simply blew the wrinkles out of a heart that had grown a bit stodgy with the protections it had taken on over the sheer sameness of the ordinary demands of daily living. The almost rapturous sight stayed with me the rest of the day. I wanted to tell everyone I ran into what I had seen, servers in our favorite restaurant, bank tellers, in effect, everyone who couldn't escape me. Pleasantly, they obliged me, and maybe I was able to pass on a little vicarious tremble to them. But others felt it too. All day long, in conversations and on news tapes, one could hear, "It's so cool...It's so cool!"

Will my life be dramatically different? Will my days and nights be all changed around? I think not. Certainly I slept easily that night and did not even dream of what I had seen. And there are the demands and habits of daily life that need me and also stabilize and bring me the comforts of focus. What did make a change in me that will never dim is the freshly-minted awareness that I still have the ability to be utterly, completely and undisguisedly amazed. That light will never again go out.

On Knowing

I believe that we cannot un-know what we know, but we can unlearn what we have been taught. There is a distinction between them, and a mighty one. Anyone with any spiritual curiosity at all feels that he stands on something larger than himself. This is what I call an inner "knowing." It cannot be taught; it cannot be withheld; it can only be uncovered, and it lies in wait, so to speak, for us to become aware of it. Everybody's got it. This knowing is essential to everything that lives, and people who count on it have no problem in paying attention to it. It seems to show up in animals whose closeness to nature guarantees it as an instinct of some sort, and it seems to be highly present in little kids who aren't yet fully constrained by the demands of the intellect.

On the other hand, learning is another ballpark altogether. Learning can enhance our knowing, of course, but it can also sideline us onto other tracks completely. The futurist, Buckminster Fuller, used to be concerned that children should not be civilized too much. He was concerned that a child's naturalness could be snared by too much contrived learning. All the careful fingering I learned as a child being taught to play the piano seems to have been overridden by pianists who know better. It almost goes without saying that sometimes we have all had to jettison entire bodies of knowledge we were taught, only to find that new perspectives have opened whole new vistas. And giving up things we thought we knew is no fun at all. I think the mind likes its habits and memories and wants to remain comfortable in them. I'm happy with my platitudes and play-things, and it is only with great effort that I will move off a treasured position to consider another. But this is learning for you...often shifty and sometimes inaccurate.

To me, inner knowing is an inherent if not preferred knowl-edge. I have spent much time with people who really know what is right for them, but they just aren't listening. The inglorious term for this is "gut feeling," no doubt. Guts or no, there is that place in us that we should listen to. Of course if we're worked up about something, there won't be a good listening until we are settled. The 19th Century scholar, Thomas Troward, reminds us to beware of "groundless fancies." These are the tricks the mind plays when it wants its own way. But let's be fair; the knowing part of us and the learning part of us are still both parts of us, and we ignore the one to the detriment of the other. I think self-aware people know that intuitive and intellectual knowing can let us reach for the skies. It only falls to us to discover what we can do with each.

On the Little Pearls

To get out of bed in the morning is to stir the flow of life in me. To head for a bit of breakfast, be it in the kitchen or my favorite corner restaurant, is to engage the morning routine that reminds me that the day has begun. I have spiritual routines that I enter into as well, and eventually every part of me, body and mind, is brought into clear awareness. I call these the "little pearls," the small, seemingly mundane thoughts and actions that orient me toward the demands of the day, maybe something like a gantry awaiting the rocket I might be ready to fire.

Night owls, no doubt, have their own set of pearls, perhaps entirely different than mine but similar insofar as they enter their folks into the stream of vital living. Night owls or day breakers, makes no difference, there is that in us that thrives on the familiar and slips into its ready flow. Looking always for the startling and exciting may give us a constant edge, but it is of little help when what we need is to settle ourselves and find a directive focus.

I needed such a focus and flow several years when I was facing a serious operation. The news of this came upon me quickly, and I found myself thrashing around for awhile. Fear seized me, and then dismay over what might happen as a result of the procedure. All the usual "What ifs" came into play, and I was irritated and confused for a time. But then my little pearls, my equalizers, began to kick in, the first of which was the prayer practice associated with my belief system. Prayer, to me, has always been a mighty settling agent in times of trouble because it helps me bring into view the spiritual basis from which I conduct my life. I had a place to stand, a foundation on which my life rested, which made this pearl a real gem. Then there were all the daily beckonings that needed attention, the small tasks that became quiet, gathering joys. I found breathing spaces, mental constructs that helped me begin to think more clearly and not just ball up into a miasma of fear. Then I went into "training." I prayed; I walked every day; I paid bills; I cooked: I talked with family and friends. Eventually the operation came and went, and I was able over time to place it in my private history as one of the episodes of my life.

We could all use little pearls, I think, gathering places where we can pull ourselves together in times of great stress and demand, familiar calls that move our energies into logical uses. There is a lot of love to be found in these, a lot of thought and care in the creation of them, and sometimes the little pearls turn into real jewels, especially when we need them.

On Patience

Patience is not a gift. It is an earned run. It is definitely a learned skill, and we all know this. Not one of us, I am sure, has ever known a patient baby. They all want what they want right now, right now, right now! When I try to capture the nature of patience, I come up with a very simple idea: Be still, and wait. Be still, and wait for the bus; be still, and wait for the answer; be still, and wait for your food to settle. Simple. Or it used to be. With the new technologies that cause us to expect more and sooner, our capacities to practice patience become less. What might have taken hours or days to be revealed, we can now pull up on a computer within minutes.

Once it was "labor-saving devices" that made the house-wife's day easier. How wonderful was the dishwasher! And it was because we could use our physical energies in other areas. We're not concerned with saving labor any more; we are interested in capturing time and expending it in the ways we choose. Imagine...trapping time...not waiting for anything...doing our purchasing, playing videos, accessing on-line libraries any time we like...turning our nights to daytime business, if we like. We are indeed liberated from the need to be still and wait.

When I think back into the histories of the submission of the United States into a civilized country, I wonder what the long, lonely passages of unoccupied land must have been like. What did the American Indians do as they traversed the miles of plains? What did people do on the long journeys going across the miles? Did they enjoy waiting in the stillness, letting their thoughts play to them? Certainly there are still occupations that take us into solitary situations, but we can fill that time, can't we? Wouldn't cowboys have smart phones?

I worry about children who cannot read the hands on an ordinary clock face, when ordinary knowledge is relegated to the dust bin. I am concerned that we are not spending time with ourselves in some nice, nothing silences. I think that sometimes our best informants are our own thoughts, but how can they make their ways to us if we make no space for them? There are vast mind stretches in us that need elongations in our days, when the flow of time all by itself can bring to us mental flights we have never before considered. When was the last time we really had a bright idea? When was a tiny spot of unknowing allowed to bubble up into a recognizable pos-sibility? Being still and waiting is the landscape for this, but because it has receded into an unused muscle, it will need to be re-discovered as a fine art.

On Buried Treasure

We all carry within us something I like to call "buried trea-sure," hidden troves of memories, senses, and feelings that take up lots of room in the recesses of our minds. In fact we lug around way more buried treasured that we do revealed trea-sure because it takes only a moment for something current to become a memory. Nothing the matter with that unless that which is buried is not sparkling silver and gold but loads of heated, bleeding recollections that simply await the chance to leap into the forefronts of our minds. Not a single shovel is needed, only the right word or image, and there we are, in pain and anger all over again.

Many of us do not even consciously think about this. We simply find ourselves at the mercy of some dark memory that springs to mind before we know it, and now we are marinating once more in the seduction of feelings made fresh again. Usually it is pirates we think of who bury things with the thought that one day they will come and gather them again. But in the human mind, it isn't pirates who bury, it's pirates of memory who steal from our present possibilities, overlaying them with rotting corpses of dead stuff that never seems to lie quietly in neat graves. Some have names, such as Unforgiveness, Hated Upbringings, Perceived Injustices, and Stolen Chances. They may well have been real once, but now they are dead, or maybe not. Maybe they are more like zombies, not alive, but not dead either.

Of course these treasures are not the only ones. There are others which hold remembered successes, beloved life episodes and valuable, learned lessons that we can pull up at will whenever we desire. But so often we go more willingly to the tough ones, the ones that hurt the most, and we have to wonder why. Does remembered pain seem more real than remembered joy? Is it somehow more... interesting? Reason would say no, but we are not only creatures of reason. We carry in us the unreasonableness of feelings as well. And, frankly, some of these remembered feelings are not even our own. Some we have never experienced ourselves but took on from stories we were told by families or from cultural backgrounds. We don't know them, but they hurt and inflame all the same. And it also means that we are subject to someone else's yesterdays, not even our own.

How to live an authentic life, how to mine the golden treasures that we ourselves accrued and put away for future use? This, I would think, is what is front and center for us. What is it that needs to remain in the ground of memory, and what can stand as a light to our way? We don't have to continue to dig over the same ground. We have a mountain of buried treasure within us, and we can choose where to look.

On Beauty

Is there something to be said for the old platitudes, "Beauty is as beauty does" or "Beauty is in the eye of the beholder?" At the very least these colloquialisms tell us that beauty is not a hard fact. Much as we might like to, we cannot set up a forever group of data about what is beautiful and what is not because we are continuing to grow into concepts of beauty we would never have imagined decades ago. How much different is today's beauty queen from her sister of fifty years ago? She's not just a skinny, blue-eyed blonde anymore. She also has deep brown orbs and ebony skin; she enjoys sleek black hair and almond-shaped eyes. And she is beautiful. Depends on who's looking and from what perspective. And these are just tiny factions in the whole thinking about beauty.

There are entire cultures of women who are completely covered from view from the world, seen uncovered only by the most private family members. Certainly concepts of beauty pervade these cultures and must surface in ways completely foreign to us. Perhaps they can be found in the presentation of a magnificent meal or the grace displayed in service. And what of the idea of "more" beautiful and "less" beautiful? Are these really accurate gauges or will beauty always be a perception rather than a decision?

We haven't even begun to think about the beauty that appears unaware, unexpected, not even contemplated... something or someone or some act that shows up to fill a moment to overflowing with an essence so lovely we are caught in a suppressed spill of tears...perhaps something not even seen...something so deep and visceral that its arrival seems completely natural, if surprising. The beauty of the innocent strikes me in this way. The tiny child is born and for a very brief while is devoid of deceptive complexities. "What you see is what you get," at least for a time, until civilization and foxing the old folks begin to turn up.

Courage carries its own beauty, active and uncompromising. We know of course about the valorous acts of people in the military, for which they should and do receive awards, even though the receivers often do not know why they should be singled out. But courage is not confined to a battlefield, at least not one on a foreign shore. Some battlefields can be found in a boardroom, a work circumstance or a household living room. There is a surge of necessity that arises in the demeanor of the one, with heart beating wildly, who speaks the words that must be spoken...and there is beauty flaring in it too.

For the spiritually inclined, there is unalloyed beauty in sidling up to the Companion. The fabulousness of the find of belonging to That Which Never Leaves cannot be weighed, measured or equated in anyway. It cannot be said; it cannot be known; it cannot be described. It is simply too beautiful to be anything but experienced. Unspeakable...unknowable...but entirely beautiful.

On Love

Is it even possible to write about the thing that makes the world go 'round in a mini-essay? Can a few words hope to capture the grandest essential in all life? I will not turn to great tomes or treatises here. They would be too cumbersome. I cannot gather up the complexities of love lost and love found in a page or two, but perhaps it is possible to capture the heart of it in every day acts, some high extensions and other mundane movings along because I do not imagine such a living, permeating thread being absent from any part of our lives, even if we cannot always find it. For some, love is synonymous with God; it is that inclusive.

Does falling in love constitute more than the chemical desire of an organic get together? Does falling out of love means we didn't know what we had in the first place? Or is all of it an exercise in discovery, some sexual, some not? How can something so much a part of our natures seem so complicated? If love is more than behaviors toward one another and more like a flowing fire that energizes everything that lives, it would seem that greater self understanding would be the order of the day if we are to have a clue to what we have within us. We could ask: if I have no idea of the love energy within me, if I cannot drink it up as part of my personal sense of well being, how can I possibly share healthy, vital, constructive love with anyone else? Good question...and one that must be answered. We cannot not use love; we can only misuse it.

It does not take rocket science to figure out how love manages itself. Nature undisturbed is a wonderful teacher. It is always in a creative mode, growing, birthing, taking care of its most vulnerable subjects. Nature looks for opportunities to express itself. Actually it is "unnatural" for it to hold back. It may wait until the time is right, but then it will not be hindered. Even when nature feeds upon itself, there is no hatred in this. There is simply the parlaying of forms from the lesser to the greater...always to more expressiveness, which, I believe, is the capstone of love in action. When love is realized in the finest of forms, there is no need for absorption, only the incredible joy of love shared.

Religion seeks it in the association of God in man. Science seeks it in the workings of the cosmos. All seek the felt connection, even though the methods may be different. I think that love finds its most magnificent earthly acts in human beings who realize that love is always present, to be utilized in consensual agreement for the greatest possible good for all. Then the eyes of the beloved will be found everywhere we look, and nothing and no one will be found wanting.

On Emergencies

When emergencies occur, everything that can get complicated will get complicated, not to mention the frequent fear that suddenly surfaces to make clear thinking difficult. Emergencies are so called because they are not on the program. They are not supposed to happen in the first place and when they do, you and I must deal with them. Obviously there are categories of emergencies, some no more than an annoying re-arrangement of time and schedules because of a flat tire that slows everything. On the other hand there are the emergencies that money can't cure and status can't prevent...a sudden loss of equilibrium, a tightening around the heart, a rush of blood from a gash or cut, injuries sustained in an auto accident. These emergencies that involve an assault on the physical well being can cause an upsurge of sudden panic and the wild wonderment on what to do next.

The mind, though, has its wonderful capacity to settle in—if we will let it—and quell the tendency to freak out. If we are the ones in need, there really are situations and people on hand for us, especially if some forethought has made us aware of them. Emotions may be high but they don't have to tear us to pieces, especially if there is a household to support us. If we are the helpers, there are good things to be said for having a few miles on us when the need to make immediate decisions face us. Being older does not guarantee good sense, but it may have already given us some practice.

It helps to be a believer of some sort, particularly when it comes to emergencies. I, for one, think that a spiritual system practiced regularly engages us in the vagaries of the day in ways that let us navigate its sometimes thrashing waters. When emergencies arise, a valued belief system gives us a place to stand during a time of tumult. I find a particularly endearing verse in the Old Textament that reads, "O rest in the Lord; wait patiently for him." Whatever one believes, the imagery here suggests some inner ground in us which is unplowed, with no furrows, no broken spots, just a place of invitation offered to the human soul, and in the acceptance there is refreshment, even in the midst of hard times.

Perhaps the greatest experience of trust in a believer's heart comes about when there is absolutely nothing physical he or she can do in an important emergency. The circumstance may be at a distance or it may be completely out of the hands of those closely involved. There may also be impending loss that cannot be averted by anyone. Still, there is a solid strength that lies in wait for us when we have to face and deal with an emergency, and this brings a gift of self knowing that cannot be found in any other way. Years ago I came to believe that every dark difficulty holds a hidden blessing. I still do.

On Getting Old and Getting Older

The fact is that we will all get older. However it is not an established fact that we will all get old. You'd think that getting older and getting old are natural courses in life, and you might think that they irrevocably belong together, but this would be a mistake for this simple reason: Getting older is a journey through time; getting old is a settled state of mind, which shows up in a body that obligingly settles along with it. Getting old is an expectation; getting older is an adventure. At the end of the day they can end up together but for anyone who wants to see where the river turns around the bend, they will not.

Are we playing with words here? Are we just trying to fool ourselves into thinking we are not denying something inevitable? I don't think so. I believe that self awareness and thinking patterns more often dictate the ways in which our lives proceed than does the simple passage of time. As I put my feet on the floor every morning I awaken, I tell myself that there have to be good reasons for getting older. It is, as I said, a fact but there are also tremendous gifts in its wings. Youth, as valued and longed for as it is, has some real limitations, one thing being perspective. When our youthful hearts are broken and disappointments seem like devastations, we feel we will never recover. A few more years of getting banged around and surviving give us more of a sense that we will manage whatever comes along....and so we do.

There is nothing the matter in living to great age (Consider the alternative!) unless somewhere in here we give up our power to others. Needing physical help is one thing; letting others do for us what we can do for ourselves is another. Most certainly there is wisdom in knowing when to relinquish some regular daily practices as needed, such as driving. This takes not only courage but also a sense of self. My dear mother as she grew older regularly bemoaned the fact that she was not as physically strong and able to do what she once did. She saw herself as being less valuable, less useful to her family, never fully realizing that her presence and the person she had become over time was what we all loved and revered—not the doing but the being that she was.

I think there is a consistent, inner perusal that older people need to make as time marches on, clear eyed and honest about how skilled we remain in some ways...and how unskilled in others. Learning is not a characteristic given only to the young. Consider the grandpas and grandmas who have returned to school to crown their lives with new knowledge. There may be an end game in getting old. There isn't one in getting older.

On Hair

I think that hair is one of the great mysteries of life. Certainly it is meant to cover heads as a form of protection from the cold, but this appears not to be uniformly true. I, for instance, have a fine, sufficient head of hair, while my sainted husband has none and must protect his vaunted top with a cap. Mostly the hairless among us are men while women go merrily through life with their thatches undiminished. However God seems to have an appropriate punishment designed for the arrogant, hoary-headed female. Imagine the horror of waking up to a bad hair day! It is at such times that we ladies discover that hair is an entirely separate entity masquerading as part of our bodies, but with a complete mind of its own. It follows no directions, gives way to no amount of ministrations and totally does exactly what it wants to do. It is at such times that women begin to entertain murderous thoughts, such as taking a pair of scissors and whacking the whole mess off!

To add to the great hair mystery it would seem that most of the favored heads belong to men... those that have hair, that is. Who is it that are born with fulsome, curly heads of hair and don't really give a damn about how their hair looks? Why, men, of course! And who is it that would perish to have such glorious curls and are instead usually plagued with saggy, limp locks that stay firmly plastered to the sides of their heads? Or such unruly hair that it sticks up all over the place? Why, women, of course! But then we are not completely without help. In fact an entire industry has grown up around the care and improvement of women's hair, probably beginning around the time the Pharoahs ruled in Egypt. What with beauty salons, hot oil treatments and permanent hair dyes, women can pretty well make it until the next dye job is needed.

Then there is whole business about baldness, as I said earlier, mostly concerning men. If they get really bummed out over their chrome domes, men can get themselves artfully-made toupees or perhaps hair transplants, a lately-come addition for the non-hirsute. There are, of course, the few who come to enjoy the appearance of greater intelligence and wisdom that the unencumbered pate gives. Ah, what secrets lie beneath that shiny egg? As a wise man once said: God only made a few perfect heads. On the rest He put hair!

Actually it seems a something of a shame to give over real time to such bit of whimsy, but then, what better way to play with a few thoughts on a sleepy, Sunday morning?

On Remembering

Lately I have been trying to remember what it felt like to fall in love, and I mean falling in love, not being in love. I have been in love with the man of my heart for what seems like forever. I'm just trying to recall a little of the unbridled insanity that goes with the heart's discovery that another rules the day. Where is he? How is he? When will I see him? Why does ordinary time seem to move so slowly, and why do I feel so out of control? Come to think of it, perhaps that is a path best not tracked. Maybe today's steadfastness is quite enough for now.

But fog horns... now there's a memory worth bringing up. Recently and very surprisingly, I heard two horn bursts out in the bay, two only, in the midst of a low-clinging, dense fog, and the experience brought back childhood memories of living near San Francisco bay and being subject to many days of dense, winter fog. Then the fog horns literally sang to one another, sometimes from the west side of the bay and sometimes eastward. I thought they were wonderful, and I could imagine all the ships being directed out of harm's way because of the magic lure of the horns. I still live near the bay, but the music of the horns has been long gone, overtaken, no doubt, by the technologies that guide ships without the need for the grand sounds. I miss that sometimes, or perhaps I miss a simplicity that has given way to the more elaborate.

Trips down Memory Lane can be a ready diversion from the things that demand our attention right now, but perhaps we shouldn't hurry down that path too often or too seriously. Sweet memories can be a comfort, sometimes too inviting a comfort when what lies in front of us seems difficult. Unpleasant memories can be like beasts lying in a corner, waiting to leap out and pounce on us when we are vulnerable, and these often come with full-blown stories of anger and regret, useless when we think of it. Who by soaking in an unhappy memory can change what happened anyway?

Now that I think about it, today with its many minutes will become a memory in no time at all...quite literally. The past may linger, but the present never does. Having completed its miraculous minute, it marches on quite relentlessly to take its place in our memories, thought about for a time, only to make its way to the hidden vaults of the mind...dragged out if need be or left to its quiet resting place.

Perhaps we should fight to stay present more than we do, to milk every moment of every drop of meaning so that it does not drift away unnoted and unused. Who needs memory when we don't even know how it got there? Memories, remembrances, yes, when they are wrought from days fully worn out from participation.

On San Francisco

Most of us have a city of our dreams, a city that lies in our imaginations as a place we long to see, perhaps even containing a kind of magical allure. Not me. The city of my dreams is San Francisco, the city where I was born and in which I grew up to young womanhood. At this point in my life I have seen many other places, some quite astonishing such as Paris, France, with the Eiffel Tower, and the amazing city in the water, Venice, Italy. But they are not San Francisco.

I am not like some who can pick up and move at the drop of a hat. Actually I admire such people's being so flexible that they can set up shop wherever they land. Me...I like my nest; I like coming through the front door and knowing what will greet me. I like being able to walk through a dark house and never run into the furniture. I like having a house that has become a home because of the generations of young ones who have grown up there and gone on their ways, coming back from time to time to take comfort in their origins. In a way I have come to feel like an old Buddha, a collector of wise searches, a dispenser of ideas and possibilities. I know which ones are mine, and I know what belongs to others to seek out. If I can open a door, both physically and metaphorically, I feel more equipped to do so somehow when I am sitting near my fireplace. Perhaps this is all a part of my imagination, but in so many ways, it works for me.

I do not live in the city of my dreams any longer, but I, like Tony Bennett, left my heart there. When during the late 80's it was beset by a major earthquake, I felt deeply for its concerns—for the people injured and undone, of course, but also for the very streets and buildings themselves. It seems childish to think of it not right that nature should wreak damage there any more than in any other place, but some things of the heart do not lend themselves to reason.

I have not seen the house where I was born in many decades, could not I even if I wanted to because it no longer exists. I do think of the home where I spent my growing-up years which does exist, and the home where some of my children were born when I was a young wife and mother. Actually I have no interest in revisiting any of it because I know the difference between a dream and real living. Perhaps we all need a place in which to memorialize our hopes, longings and inspirations, a place that once existed—in whole or in part—which gives a sense of our own beginnings. Most of us don't or can't live in that actual spot any more, but that is not important. What matters is the recognition of a point of origin. Good, bad or otherwise, it says, here I once stood.

On Texting

The other day I ran across a quote attributed to Albert Einstein, to wit: "It has become appallingly obvious that our technology has exceeded our humanity." Naw, I thought, that's just too extreme. The old coot must have been having a bad day when he said that. Then I thought about texting, which Einstein might never have imagined. God...maybe the old bird was right. And he has been gone since 1955.

Don't get me wrong. Texting can be wonderful for trying to catch someone on the way home. Touch...touch...brng hom the buttr...touch...touch... pik up the clening. And we cannot put aside the boon that text messaging is to the deaf. But spending much of the day growing calluses on your thumbs? I have watched couples sitting across from one another in a restaurant texting throughout an entire meal. I have ridden in a car with teenagers who never looked up from their cell phones during the entire drive. Worse, we all know of drivers who ran into and killed pedestrians because they did not see them as they were texting...make that, reading...while driving. Are we missing something here? Was old AE right when he complained about the overlay of technology on our humanity?

We could ask: What happens when a device meant to be energy saving becomes an integral part of the way we live our lives? Was texting ever meant to take the place of real, face-to-face conversations or at least a caring voice on the telephone? Can we really convey great love or deep sadness through unpunctuated, shorthand lettering on the screen of a cell phone? My business is spiritual counseling, and I've been wondering how I might conduct an interaction through text messaging. Maybe something like...hey grl how r u my hrt is brken my dog died O 2 bad i wl txt u a pryer. Don't think this would work out too well. What part of being human could we be giving up by shorthanding our communications to one another?

We can never go back from using the new, the faster, the more enhanced. We cannot unknow what we know, but we can think again about how to keep our hearts in the forefront of our lives. We spend years teaching a child how to become more skilled at living a civilized life, about discovering what morality means and what compassionate thinking does for the human condition. Using a cell phone, a child can pull up the weather conditions in Caracas, Venezuela, but he cannot experience the expressed love shown in holding another's hand in comfort. Only the extended hand can do this.

We're smart folks. We can remember once more what electronic and digitized communication can do, and what it cannot. An e-mail cannot adequately convey the heart's love. Certainly a text message cannot either.

On Meekness

In the 5th Chapter of Matthew, the New Testament, the Master uttered a series of beautiful, aphoristic statements called The Beatitudes. Among them, there is one that always puzzled me: Blessed are the meek, for they shall inherit the earth. Made no sense to me, considering what we usually think of as meekness. I think of meek types as those who hunker down in a corner somewhere, staying out of the way, the ones who don't make waves, the ones who manage to stay away from the blows. How can such people inherit the earth, and what would they do with it if they could? Give it away to the first bully who comes along?

Obviously I was missing something here. Such inheritances had to involve more than tracts of land on the planet... more like gardens of wisdom found in the mind. We are not talking about physical things as much as frames of mind, and when I read Emmett Fox's thoughts on this parable, I saw a new, healthy meaning. We can think of meekness as a form of openness to the Divine Good, a release of personal stubbornness so that we may be taught; we may learn. What a wonderful mental pliability there is that lets us take in fresh revelations rather than be completely consumed with my-way-or-the-highway-thinking!

These days we are bombarded with information which blasts the senses with speed and volume. From a technological point of view I suppose it is highly desirable to be able to access facts at an instant. What I wonder about is our willingness to explore the facts to see if they are worthy of our time and energy, or are they things in the mist that fly from us as quickly as they come? And what of facts? How much life is there in the facts of our lives as in the senses that do not qualify as facts but as "knowings," openings, mental expansions, and insights that are often ineffable? What is it that really influences us...the columns of facts that are churned out with every news cycle (if we stay awake long enough to notice them), or the guidances that urge us from within ourselves? The meek fellow within us is not out there world beating as much as allowing for new ways of thinking and working.

I have to imagine that people in "think tanks" do exactly that...think. I could not say whether they are contentious about their work together or not, but I figure that somewhere in what they do there are the means for doors to open and let in surprises. Otherwise they'd be hashing and re-hashing the same stuff.

The Master may have brought up some familiar wisdoms from Jewish lore, but he always had a new "take" on them. We know he could get upset and worked up, but it was his meek side that held his light. I would think that having a meek corner in our homes for contemplation would do us good, maybe even more than a workout at the gym.

On a Rosy Dawn

There is nothing so newly born as a rosy dawn after the night winds blow gently and leave a little particulate matter in the atmosphere. It brings the look of my own infant children back to me every time I see one. I think that nature works overtime on these, as if we humans have been doing enough good things for a while that we deserve a reward.

These dawns come in my neck of the woods when the cold morning air is chiseled away from the darkness, anticipating the sunrise. It's a tricky procedure. If the sun shows too vigorously the dawn clouds dissipate too quickly. But if, however, the night skies cling just a little longer before giving way to morning, the magic mixing of sun, clouds and night combine so that the skies bleed from magenta to rose to soft pink, in motion all the time. With every shift of coming daylight, tiny tips of clouds vacate color, only to be replaced by a new hue, sometimes faint, sometimes more intense. I have to keep looking, oh, I have to, for the radiance slips away before my eyes as the morning sun eventually claims the heavens for its own. This panoply of unbridled splashing lasts minutes...just minutes, and then it is gone until the next time. I love these dawns, and I'm always sorry to see them leave, but I don't miss them. I don't want to grab them on a lens to make them stay because I know there will be others.

I think that maybe this willingness to let the beauty go allows it to be more precious to me while it lingers. Some beautiful things...or situations...or people...are simply not going to be around forever. They seem meant to grace us for awhile and then make their ways to something or somewhere else. If we are wise we will languish in their loveliness while they are with us and not waste time being regretful when they leave. We can try to bring up a memory, but even these are skewed the next time a beautiful thing flits before our eyes again. And who by plumbing memory can bring forth the sensuousness of Ravel's Bolero without the need to hear those strains again?

We can and do capture beauty permanently so that many eyes can see it. There is no question that Michelangelo's heroic David or the soulful Pieta' capture our hearts whenever we see them. Only now these magnificent works must be protected... from us, who would attack them with hammers! We can no longer hope to touch a fine, marble, curved finger again. This makes me sad, and it makes me think that maybe my ephemeral dawns evoke more joy in me. They may not last long, but they will be back, and no one can harm them.

On Forgetting and Remembering

People who are spiritually curious can find a world of systems to investigate, and they often do. Many years ago a friend of mine whimsically said that we are looking for the 4 "Ps"...parking places, princes, palaces and prosperity...and that assessment has stood up very well over time. Some people weave their ways in and out of spiritual endeavors, often saying, "not this." But others, more soul involved, find a belief that is both inspiring and pragmatic; it satisfies the intuitive level of exploration but also presents very hands-on ways to go. And these people can spend a lifetime in the practices that they have come to love.

I know the belief system that holds my heart, and at the same time I have visited many others with friends. Are some better than others, I am asked? In answer to this I would have to say that, as long as there is freedom to choose without restraint, all will present a view that works for some. What I have come to believe is that, whatever our beliefs may be, as people practicing that which we accept as spiritual truth for us, we are, bottom line, doing one of two things: We are either remembering who we are as spiritual beings, or we are forgetting. In fact we are in one or the other of these states all day long...often without even thinking about it. For example, let's say that you, the reader, completed a quiet morning's prayer and contemplation, feeling good, ready to go, all fired up. You then get in your car and head out. Once on the freeway someone cuts in a little too closely, and you have to slow down suddenly. What often happens next is that you begin to entertain "exotic" thoughts about the inconsiderate driver and maybe even flash an equally exotic hand gesture! Oops! What happened? First you were tooling along all spiritually revved...and then you got sidetracked and forgot who you were. (Certainly you forgot who the other driver was also!) Happens all the time in so many ways. The demands of the world cannot help us. The conditions of our lives need our attention and cannot be expected to support our spiritual prowess.

It is we who through our sweet practices and chosen focus bring us once more into a place of remembering our essential spirituality. No need to lacerate ourselves for falling away from what we believe. There is much too much energy spent in a full-on regimen of self laceration that will never get us where we want to go. It is enough to simply self correct, remember ourselves as Beloveds of God, and get on with

the business of living vital, spiritual lives. A wise philosopher said that God turns to us as we turn to God. There is no
question of being refused the Divine Energies. They move
through us always, whether we are always wise in our use of
them or not. This is what Oneness means.

On The "Other"

In my neighborhood there is an old, Asian man who walks several of the streets regularly. I can't set my watch by him, but I can just about figure when he'll show up because he takes a lap around our breakfast coffee shop about the time we arrive. If we are seated by the window looking out at the sidewalk, he will stop, and remain stopped, until we acknowledge him with a wave and a smile, and then shuffle on. I have made up a story about him. I imagine him as an old Tibetan monk, always carrying a string of prayer beads with him and waving them as he goes. Once I happened to be outside the restaurant as he was walking by, and I tried to engage him in some talk, but was completely unsuccessful. He could only smile, utter some strange syllables and seem abashed that I had made the effort. And so he remains the "other," someone not of my clan, my tribe, my community, destined to remain a stranger.

This "otherness" is not as remote as my little incident suggests. We can live in this even among the neighbors in close proximity to us, and there is no real surprise in this. Unless one lives on a quiet cul-de-sac where householders throw out-door parties for themselves, we can go for long periods with-out even knowing the names of any neighbors except those on either side of us, or, if we are apartment dwellers, maybe the ones we'll commonly share the elevator with.

I guess there should be no mystery here. So many of our interests have become insular, what with the closedness we can develop through technologies. TV's and computers can fill the hours in the day quite nicely. We can text and tweet without ever having to utter a single, spoken word, and work cubicles can secure us from too many invaders. When I worked in an office setting a half century ago, there was a whole array of people out on the floor together, which necessitated a certain amount of convivial conversation. From my desk I could look up and see my boss sitting only a few feet from me. This was togetherness, and we all shared the available space. Not anymore... and I suspect that a certain amount of our now-ingrained alienation has come from the lack of need to physi-cally connect.

When he was trying to assist the Israelis and Palestinians make peace, then President Bill Clinton spoke of the "easy habits of hatred" and the "hard tasks of reconciliation." I think he seized upon a great truth, and not just for the war-ring Middle East. It is easy, so easy, to hate and distrust the "other" because we simply do not know him. It is no wonder it becomes so hard to break through the habits of dismissiveness and myth telling.

After many decades of knowing my neighbors across the street, I lately watched that family finally move away and a new neighbor move in. The house itself is on the "up" side of the hill while ours is on the "down" side. I think I'll need to make the trek up that long flight of stairs to introduce myself.

On Incivility

When I was a kid I was taught manners, which seems today to be something that belongs on another planet. Many people seem to think of manners as some kind of artificial contrivance to "make nice," which is missing the point entirely. As cute and lovable as babies are, they have the general demeanor of wild animals until and unless they are gently taught over time to become aware that there are others in this life besides themselves who want consideration and attention. When these subtle trainings aren't present, children can grow up with no sense of boundaries or behaviors that will help them get along with others, especially their own cohorts. Whacking the kid next to you in day care because you want his toy is not going to cut it for very long, and it becomes really tough on a little fellow if he can't handle himself in kindergarten. In the long run the neglect of even the barest of civilizing techniques breeds a generation of people who are basically uncivil. They seem neither to know how to restrain themselves or care, and restraint by force generates nothing except annoyance about being restrained.

It makes me very sad to engage so many people who seem lost by the expectations of some societal norms, such as waiting in line until your turn comes up or spreading a little joy by thanking someone for their efforts on your behalf. I think that some are brought up to think of themselves as special, which by extension means that others are not, and in this specialness they deserve first crack, superior treatment and are entitled to be first up in all things. And what are some of the results that go along with this specialness? Often it means miserable treatment of others without even a clue that this is happening.

I know a whole set of people who seem haplessly to walk over others, leaving a trail of broken relationships behind them and, worse, not even looking back to notice. Eventually they may become aware that they are, in many instances, vaguely missing something. If they have money and power they can command the obeisances of others, and thus surround themselves with lieutenants who nod and smile, but not anyone who willingly sticks around. They do not know that incivility kills more opportunities that it cultivates. They cannot hear the grinding teeth of those next to them who bear a quiet irritation, nor are they overly concerned about why their family members drift away from them.

What does come home...finally...silently...pushing through the blind denials of their own culpabilities...is the fact that they are unloved and not missed. Incivility long ago destroyed all vestiges of kindness and genuine loving concern. One might hope that in some errant dream, Marley's ghost might pay a visit before it is really too late for clanking chains to get their attention.

On Wholeness

Students of spirituality are enamored with the entire concept of wholeness. Just the largeness of the word itself invites the thinker to embrace unknown elements of life that we may not yet imagine. To me, wholeness has a much broader scope than holiness, although I don't consider it particularly secular. Wholeness simply suggests that nothing can be added, nothing taken away, and this takes in our religions, our atheisms, our grand successes and our dismal failures. If wholeness is the pristine position, this must mean that sooner or later, all forms, conditions, beliefs and actions will resolve themselves into the waiting embrace of wholeness, only to be recast once more into other forms, conditions, beliefs, and actions. If we will allow it, if we let ourselves be disentangled from whatever strictures we may be clinging to, we can be made new again. Made…new…again…any time, any place, anywhere.

Does this seem so far outside the realm of human conditions that we cannot ever conceive of it? If we can, think of the freedom that lies within wholeness, the healings, the releases, the forgivenesses, the opportunities to love and be creative again. Healing lies within wholeness as an integral part of how it operates; in fact it is the path of footsteps that lead to renewal. The desire to be healed lets us know that something is off kilter and that a new track needs to be followed. Some have said that healing always awaits, and if we will allow for its unerring guidance and love energies, we will move into wholeness once more. I don't believe that healing is ever unshackled from love, and when its energies accompany any techniques we may be using, we are in healthy territory.

I think it can be difficult sometimes when we are so concerned with our physical lives to imagine that we are fully contained within an infinite quality. Sometimes it seems remote to think that something invisible, contacted within the mind, can have such a radical effect on our very humanity. Yet we know and experience this every day. Think of what being in love feels like! Not too many other things can undo the habits of a self-regulated individual in quite the way that the heights of love can.

There is a natural order in wholeness, something that tries to re-establish itself within us every chance it gets. Of course this would be so. If wholeness is a quality of the Divine Nature, it is part of ours by extension, and it will "out" itself whenever possible. Often it is enough to quit fussing and fighting with perceived obstacles and practice "letting"...letting healing take place, letting things that aren't ours to handle pass from us, letting our natural equilibrium find its place once more. We don't have to get wholeness; we simply reveal it.

On Money

I'm not sure which is the most corruptive...love, money or sex. At the end of the day I suspect it's money. Most of us do settle down with the love and sex in our experiences, but some never settle with whatever money they have. They want more, not just because they may need it for better living but because they just want it. No real reason sometimes, just more... more than my family, more than my friends, more than the next guy. My bank account must be bigger than it is. This can become terminally disruptive. The waters are never still, and the scenery is never lovely enough. Sometimes we don't even know that there is an addictive lure at work. Something just viscerally churns away in us, pushing us toward the next buck.

Don't get me wrong. I love money. I love to earn it; I love to spend it; I love to save it; I love to give it away. And unlike a lot of people, I love to carry cash, especially the new, colorized greenbacks, (the fifty-dollar bill, with the American flag waving in the background—a work of art!) If the government in its wisdom should ever do away with cash money, I would immediately go into mourning! I guess what I'm trying to say is that I know the place of money, and it does have a place in my life, but only that.

Buckminster Fuller once whimsically said that we got money because it became too hard to cut up a cow for payment. Sounds good to me. Money started out as a fabulous medium of exchange, and then things changed very quickly. Ya gotta wonder—was it the gold—or the glitter? I think that once money became an end...and an entity...in itself, it lost its real importance and took on a power that was never intended. For some, money does indeed behave like a separate entity, something just dancing out of their grasp, like the taunting, little kid that races away, shouting, "Catch me if you can." Other elements of their lives fall more readily into place but money often seems just out of reach.

Author, Michael Sandel, writes books on the moral limits that money should demonstrate in the market place. He asks what I consider a very scary question: "Why worry that we are moving toward a society in which everything is for sale?" Why, indeed, and are we really sliding down a slippery slope where the things and qualities we value more as sacred can now be sold if enough money is at stake? Should we be more personally conscious about the place money really does hold in our lives? I don't think there is any doubt about this.

Still...I've seen plenty of Benjamins in my day. I wouldn't mind seeing Grover Cleveland on a thousand-dollar bill before I die...or Woodrow either on a hundred-thousand dollar bill!